The Five Points of Presbyterianism

The Distinctives of Presbyterian Church Government

Thomas Dwight Witherspoon

GW00685839

Log College Press

www.logcollegepress.com

The Five Points of Presbyterianism:
The Distinctives of Presbyterian Church Government
By Thomas Dwight Witherspoon
© 2017 by Log College Press
First published in *Centennial of Presbyterianism in Kentucky, 1783-1883. Addresses delivered at Harrodsburg, Kentucky, October 12, 1883* (Louisville, KY: Courier Journal Print Co., 1883), as "The Distinctive Doctrines and Polity of Presbyterianism." Digital transcription by Wayne Sparkman, Director of the PCA Historical Center. Used by permission.

Log College Press
92 Cotton Wood Dr.
Madison, MS 39110
www.logcollegepress.com

Page and cover design by Clay Meyer
Printed in the USA by Hederman Brothers Printing, Madison, MS

ISBN: 978-1-948102-00-1 (booklet)

ISBN: 978-1-948102-02-5 (ePub)

ISBN: 978-1-948102-03-2 (Mobi)

INTRODUCTION

Many people are familiar with what are known as the "Five Points of Calvinism." Few people are acquainted with what Thomas Dwight Witherspoon lays out in this booklet as the "Five Points of Presbyterianism." Even among members of Presbyterian churches, these five distinctives of the Presbyterian form of church government are relatively unknown. Yet it is important for those who would align themselves with this particular expression of Christ's church to understand its nature, its claims, and its unique beauty. We publish this booklet in the confidence that all Presbyterian church members (especially officers and officer candidates), as well as those outside Presbyterianism, will benefit from Witherspoon's overview of these vital topics.

Who was Thomas Dwight Witherspoon? He was born on January 17, 1836, in Greensboro, Alabama, and was educated at the then-famous academy of Henry Tutwiler. He attended the University of Alabama, but graduated in 1856 from the University of Mississippi. Discerning a call to gospel ministry, he went to Columbia Theological Seminary in South Carolina to study under James Henley Thornwell, John Bailey Adger, Aaron Leland, and George Howe. After graduating in 1859, he returned to his college town of Oxford, Mississippi, to become the pastor of its Presbyterian church. When the American Civil War started in 1861, however, he left the pastorate to enter the Confederate Army as a private. He soon became a Chaplain of the Second and the Forty-Second Mississippi Infantry and was in active service at the battle of Gettysburg. There he was captured and spent several months as a prisoner of war at Fort McHenry in Baltimore.

Following the Civil War, Witherspoon served as the pastor of Second Presbyterian Church in Memphis, Tennessee (1865-1870); the pastor of the Presbyterian church in Christiansburg, Virginia (1870-1870); the chaplain at the University of Virginia (1871-1873); the pastor of Tabb Street Presbyterian Church in Petersburg, Virginia (1873-1882); the pastor of First Presbyterian Church in Louisville, Kentucky (1882-1891); and the pastor of First

Presbyterian Church in Richmond, Kentucky (1881-1894). His final call was as the Professor of Homiletics and Pastoral Theology at the newly formed Louisville Presbyterian Theological Seminary. He ministered there until his death on November 3, 1898.

Dr. Witherspoon, who served as Moderator of the General Assembly of the Presbyterian Church in the United States in 1884, was a useful and influential minister of the gospel of the Lord Jesus Christ. He was remembered as a kind, respectable, and insightful professor, especially popular with young men. He published numerous articles and sermons, as well as two books (*Children of the Covenant* in 1873 and *Romanism* in 1881). The Thomas Dwight Witherspoon papers, including unpublished sermons and biographical information on which this sketch is based, are housed at the PCA Historical Center (http://www.pcahistory.org/findingaids/witherspoon).

These words were first an address given at Harrodsburg, Kentucky, on October 12, 1883, at the centennial celebration of Presbyterianism in Kentucky. Given the nature of Witherspoon's audience and the occasion of delivery, he does not spend as much time grounding his statements in the Scriptures as he might have done in a treatise prepared for publication. Those who desire to study this subject further are encouraged to read, among many other books we could recommend, Thomas Witherow's nineteenth century classic *The Apostolic Church: Which Is It?*, which traverses much the same ground as Witherspoon, though in a different order. Witherow also adds a sixth point that Witherspoon presupposed—Jesus Christ alone is the King and Head of His church.

May King Jesus use this booklet to cause His people to become more convinced of, and more enamored with the beauty of, the Biblical form of church government called Presbyterianism.

CALEB CANGELOSI

MADISON, MS

THE FIVE POINTS OF PRESBYTERIANISM

Every denomination of Christians has certain distinctive principles, which serve to differentiate it from other branches of the visible Church, and which constitute its *raison d'être*—the ground more or less substantial of its separate organic existence. In proportion as these principles are vital and fundamental, they vindicate the body that becomes their exponent from the charge of faction or schism, and justify its maintenance of an organization separate and apart from that of all who traverse or reject them.

We are met today as Presbyterians. We have come to commemorate the first settlement of Presbyterianism in Kentucky. You have listened to the eloquent addresses of those who have traced the history of our Church in this commonwealth for a hundred years. They have told you of the first planting in this Western soil of a tender branch from our old and honored Presbyterian stock, of the storms it has encountered, of the rough winds that have beaten upon it, and yet of its steady growth through summer's drought and winter's chill, until what was erstwhile but a frail and tender plant, has become a sturdy oak with roots deep-locked in the soil, with massive trunk and goodly boughs and widespread branches overshadowing the land.

You have heard also, the thrilling narratives of the lives of those heroic men by whose personal ministry the Church was founded; of the toils they underwent, of the perils they encountered, of the hardships they endured that they might plant the standards of Presbyterianism in these Western wilds.

The question arises with especial emphasis under circumstances like these: What are the peculiar principles of the denomination whose centennial is celebrated with so much enthusiasm today? Is there anything in these principles that justifies such sacrifices and toils as were made by the noble men whose biographies have been read? Is there anything in the distinctive doctrines and polity of this Church to render its settlement in Kentucky a hundred years ago, and its perpetuation and development through a century of conflict and struggle, a matter worthy of such joyous, grateful commemoration as we give today? Is there anything in these creeds and symbols, venerable with years, which we have received from our forefathers, which makes them an inheritance meet to be transmitted in their integrity and purity, with increasing veneration, to our children and to our children's children forever?

These, Christian friends, are the questions that, through the kindness and partiality of my brethren, I am to endeavor to answer today. And in the fulfillment of my task, I invite you to walk with me for a little while about this, our ancestral Zion, to "mark well her bulwarks and consider her palaces that ye may tell it to the generation following."

The Distinctives of Presbyterianism

And first, let us endeavor to get a clear idea as to what constitute the distinctive principles of Presbyterianism, as to what there is that is peculiar in its doctrine and polity. Confining myself strictly under the head of doctrine, to the department of ecclesiology or the doctrine of the Church, and viewing the polity of Presbyterianism in its only proper light as basing itself distinctly upon, and adjusting itself most accurately to that form of doctrine delivered in Scripture, I may say that, just as in our doctrine of Redemption, there emerge the historical *five points*, over which controversy has waged since the days of the Synod of Dort, so in our doctrine of the Church there are five points, constituting five distinctive principles of Church government, each one of which places our Church polity in sharp contrast with that of other Churches around us, and all of which together make up a system as unique as it is beautiful, as scriptural as it is complete, having nothing comparable to it in any other organization in the world.

Let us take up these five points of Presbyterianism successively, and endeavor to engrave them as clearly as possible upon our memories and upon our hearts.

Church Power in the People

The first fundamental principle of Presbyterianism is that Church power is vested not in officers of any grade or rank, but in the whole corporate body of believers. Our doctrine is that Christ, who is the great Head of the Church, the alone fountain and source of all its power, has not vested this power primarily in a single officer who is the visible head of the Church and the vicar of Christ, as in the Roman Catholic Church, or in the body of Bishops or superior clergy as in the Episcopal Church, or in the whole body of the clergy as in the Methodist and some other churches, but in the people, the whole body of the people, so that no man can attain to any office, exercise any authority, or wield any power in the Church, except he is called to that office, invested with that authority and clothed with that power by the voice of the people.

Here, then, is a grand, fundamental difference between the Presbyterian Church and all those churches that are prelatical or hierarchical in form, in that ours is a government in which Christ rules through the voice of his people, his whole redeemed people, and not through any privileged class, any spiritual nobility, or aristocracy of grace.

Representative Rule

The second fundamental principle of Presbyterianism is that this power, though vested in the people, is not administered by them immediately, but through a body of officers chosen by them, and commissioned as their representatives to bear rule in Christ's name. The offices that are to be filled have been ordained of Christ, and none may be added to those which he has ordained. The officers who fill these offices are chosen by a vote of the whole membership of the Church over which they are to rule, and yet are to be chosen under such special prayer for the guidance of the Holy Spirit who dwells in the Church, that whilst the outward vocation to office is from the Church, the inward call and commission to each officer is to be recognized as from Christ Himself, the great invisible and spiritual head. The only power, therefore, immediately exercised by the people is this most important and fundamental power, that of vocation. They choose those who shall administer the government over them. These rulers act as their representatives and so the government is a representative government, as distinguished from a pure democracy or a government of the people by themselves.

This principle separates us from all churches that are congregational in form, as the first from all that are prelatic or hierarchical. This last distinguishes us, therefore, from the Congregational churches of England and of this country, from all churches of the Baptist faith and order, and from those churches around us that call themselves the Christian, or Reformed, in all of which questions of doctrine and discipline are decided by a direct vote of the whole congregation, whilst in ours these questions are settled by the voice of those officers who are chosen to bear rule.

One Office of Rule

The third fundamental principle of Presbyterianism is that the whole administration of government in the Church has been committed to a single order of officers, all of whom, though having in some respects different functions to perform, are of co-ordinate and equal authority in the Church. It is true that the Presbyterian Church, after the pattern of Scripture, has two orders of officers, the elder and the deacon; but the deacon is not a ruler. He has no spiritual oversight or authority. His office is purely executive. He has charge only of the secular concerns of the Church. Its government is committed to a single order of officers, the presbyters or elders. These elders are of two classes. There is first a class who, not having been called of God to be preachers of the Gospel, but recognizing His call through the Church to bear rule, continue in their secular avocations, devote such portion of their time as they can spare from their business to the oversight and care of the flock, and exercise full authority as rulers over the house of God. These are called Ruling Elders, because their office is simply to rule. There is a second class who, in addition to the call to bear rule, recognize a divine voice summoning them also to the work of preaching the Gospel, and this function of preaching, which is the highest and most honorable in the Church, demands their whole time, so that they give up secular callings, and are specially set apart of the Church to this higher function, and so are known as Teaching Elders or Ministers of the Word.

But whilst this ministry of the Word entitles them to special honor, it confers no higher rank and invests with no superior authority. The minister in our church courts has no more authority than the ruling elder, so that we not only have in the Presbyterian Church the "parity of the clergy," of which we hear so much, but the parity of the eldership, of the ruling elder with the teaching elder, a principle not to be found under any other form of church government.

Joint Rule

The fourth distinctive principle of Presbyterianism is that these Presbyters rule not singly but jointly in regularly-constituted assemblies or courts. This is a principle upon which I would lay particular emphasis; for in it the admirable genius of our system especially appears. Whilst there are functions that are purely administrative, such as preaching the Word, administering the sacraments, etc., which a Presbyter may, when so commissioned, perform separately and individually, yet all legislative and judicial functions are to be administered by assemblies or courts alone. And no one of these assemblies is competent to the transaction of any business unless representatives of both classes of Presbyters, ministers and ruling elders, are present. There is no exercise of any several authority, as by a bishop or a presiding elder, in any part of the field. There is no possibility of any one man power, for all authority must come with the sanction of a church court.

Subordinated Church Courts

The last distinctive principle of Presbyterianism is that these church courts are so subordinated to one another that a question of government or discipline may be carried by appeal or complaint or review from a lower to a higher court, representing a larger number of congregations, until every part of the Church is, through this due subordination, brought immediately under the supervision and control of the whole. Thus our Church Sessions, which constitute the lowest order of assemblies, are, as many lie within a certain district, subordinated to a higher court or Presbytery, constituted of representatives from each of these Church Sessions, meeting twice every year and oftener if necessary. The minutes of the Church Sessions all pass under the inspection of the Presbytery by way of review and control. There is the right both of appeal and complaint to the Presbytery from any action of any of these Church Sessions; and Presbytery has in such cases all the right of a higher court or court of appeals.

The same is true of the Synods in relation to the Presbyteries, and of the General Assembly in reference to the Synods—so that the authority and oversight of the whole Church is brought to bear upon every part, and the right of appeal belongs to the humblest member of the Church, by which he may carry his cause through all intermediate courts to the General Assembly, the highest of all.

Here, then, to recapitulate, is our system of government—power vested in the great body of Christ's people; administered through officers chosen by the people and commissioned of Christ; administered by a single order of officers equal in authority and rank; administered not severally but jointly, in duly organized assemblies or courts, and in assemblies or courts so subordinated to each other as to bind the whole mass together in a unity of mutual oversight, government, and control.

Such, in brief, is the system of church polity which we hold. It differs, as you will readily perceive, in its essential features from that of every other denomination. It is the system held by that great Presbyterian body, which is composed not only of the various branches of the Presbyterian Church in this country, in Canada, in England, Scotland, Ireland, and Wales, but also of what are known as the Reformed Churches of Germany, Belgium, Holland, Switzerland, France, etc., comprising in all a constituency of nearly if not altogether fifty millions of souls.

The Beauty of Presbyterianism

For this system we claim, without seeking to disparage that of any other representative body of Christians, the following points of excellence:

Its Exact Scripturalness

As Presbyterians we hold that everything concerning the doctrines and polity of the Church must be brought to the sure criterion of the Word of God. To that which is revealed nothing is to be added, and from it nothing is to be taken away. And so we hold to our form of government because we believe that essentially, in all its leading features, it is the same that was delivered by our Lord to His inspired apostles, and by them to the primitive Church. We find, from the study of the New Testament, that the apostles were accustomed to "ordain elders in every city" [Titus 1:5]. As there was but one church planted in each city these elders were, most of them, Ruling Elders. We find that, as in the 20th chapter of Acts, these officers, are in one place called elders, and in another, bishops, showing that the New Testament bishop is not a diocesan officer, but only an elder considered as having the oversight of a congregation of believers. We find that these elders, together with the deacons, constitute the only orders of permanent officers in the Church. Even the apostles themselves, recognize themselves in the exercise of authority in the Church as elders. Thus, Peter says: "I, Peter, who am also an elder and a witness," etc. [I Peter 1:5], and John, the apostle, begins his epistle: "The elder to the well-beloved Gaius," etc. [III John 1].We find that these elders are of two classes, exactly corresponding to those in the Presbyterian Church now; the "elders that rule," and "those that labor in word and doctrine" [I Timothy 5:17]. We find that their authority is exercised in duly organized courts. Timothy is ordained by the laying on of hands of a Presbytery. A Synod is convened at Jerusalem, composed of the apostles and brethren, before which is issued and decided an appeal from the Church at Antioch. Our entire system in all its five essential principles, is, therefore, found in Scripture.

Our polity is that revealed in the Word of God; and in its exact script-uralness, its close conformity to the "pattern given in the mount," is found the first great excellency of Presbyterianism. To this scripturalness of our system, we have the testimony of the ablest and most learned biblical scholars, and even of those who differ with us in forms of government. In the Episcopal Church, for instance, which lays such exclusive claim to apostolic origin and descent, the ablest scholars and the profoundest theologians admit that, in the days of the apostles, the bishops were only pastors of churches, and the present order of diocesan bishops was not known. This is the testimony of Archbishops Usher, Whately, and Tate, Bishop Lightfoot, Canon Farrar, Dean Stanley, Dean Howson, Lord Macaulay, Mr. Hallam the historian, and a host of others whom I could name, so that we justly claim for our system its strict accordance with the teachings of Scripture.

Its Vindication of the Unity of the Visible Church Under All Dispensations

The Scriptures constantly speak of the visible Church as being the same under both the old and new dispensations. Paul does not represent the olive tree as being rooted out and another planted in its stead, but as having the Jewish branches broken off, and the Gentile branches engrafted in their room. Now, under our Presbyterian theory of church government, and under it alone, have we a clear conception of this visible unity under both dispensations.

Let us look for a moment at the form of government under the old

economy. The first distinct reference we have to the Church as a visible organization is in connection with the calling of Abram, and his settlement
in Canaan. Doubtless, the visible Church had existed before, had existed
since the offering of the first sacrifice before the gates of the lost Eden—
but here is the first reference to its organic form. And now what is that
form? The only officers we read of are the elders of Abraham's house. One
of these, Eliezer, is distinctly mentioned (Genesis 24:2) as the "servant and
elder of his house" (not the eldest servant, as in the authorized version, but
the servant and elder). We hear little of these elders at this time, for we
hear little of the Church; but they are to play a very prominent part a little
later. At the time of the Exodus they appear as the distinctly-recognized
officers of the Church; when Moses is sent as the deliverer of God's people
from the bondage of Egypt, he is directed (Exodus 3:16) to go and gather
the "elders of Israel" together, and deliver his message to them, as divinely-appointed rulers of the congregation.

When he is sent to demand of Pharaoh the release of the children of
Israel, he is instructed to take with him (Exodus 3:18) the "elders of Israel,"
as the representatives of the chosen people. When in the wilderness Moses
receives the law from the hands of Jehovah, on Mount Sinai, he writes it,
and delivers it to the priests, the sons of Levi, and *the elders* (Deuteronomy
31:9) as the spiritual rulers of God's people. In every instance in which
any authority is exercised or any discipline administered, we find these
elders referred to as the rulers in the Church. They are sometimes called,
"the elders;" sometimes "the elders of Israel;" sometimes "the elders of the
congregation;" sometimes "the elders of the people;" but they appear on
every page of the history of the Jewish Church, as its divinely-appointed
and recognized rulers.

Nor was the term *elder* one simply of seniority or of respect, as some
have supposed. There were many elders in age, who were not elders in
office. The term *elder* implied official rank and position. Thus, when the

Lord directed Moses to select out of the elders of the tribes, seventy, who should constitute the highest council of the Church, or, as we might say, its General Assembly, he instructed him (Numbers 11:16) to choose only those whom he certainly knew to be "elders of the people, and officers over them."

The Jewish Church was, therefore, governed by elders in the days of Moses. It was so in the days of Joshua, when there were elders in every city (Joshua 7:6; 20:4; 24:31; etc.), and in the days of Judges (Judges 2:7; 8:16; Ruth 4:2; etc.), and in the days of Samuel (1 Samuel 15:30; 16:4; etc.), and in the days of David (2 Samuel 5:3; 17:4; etc.), and in the days of Elijah and Elisha (1 Kings 21:11; 2 Kings 6:32; etc.), and in the days of Ezekiel (Ezek. 14:1; 20:1; etc.), and in the days of Ezra, when the Old Testament canon was completed (Ezra 10:14; etc.), and in the days when our Savior appeared in the world (Matthew 21:23; 27:1; Mark 8:31; Luke 22:52; etc.).

It is sometimes asserted that these elders were only civil rulers and not ecclesiastical; officers of the State and not of the Church; that the priests had the exclusive authority in spiritual matters, and the elders in secular matters. But, so far is this from being the case, that, as we shall soon see, the priests themselves, ruled, not as priests, but as elders, and in every act of government were associated with the "elders of the people," while the council of seventy, or the Sanhedrin, as it was afterwards called, was composed entirely of elders, chosen from the different tribes of Israel. It is true, that, owing to the union of Church and State, these elders had many civil duties to perform. But their functions as civil officers, resulting from this temporary connection, were only incidental. Their highest functions were spiritual. They were pre-eminently ecclesiastical rulers. They had charge of all the interests of the "Church of God which was in the Wilderness with the angel which spake to Moses on Mount Sinai" [Acts 7:38]. The fact that they had civil duties to perform, and secular questions to decide, no more proves that they were not Church officers than does the sitting of the bishops of the established Church of England in the House of Lords prove that they are not Church officers.

The Old Testament Church was, therefore, Presbyterian, inasmuch as its whole government was administered by *elders* chosen from among the people and set apart to the office of rulers over the house of God. It was still further Presbyterian in the sense that these elders were of two distinct classes—elders of the priests and elders of the people. This appears very distinctly in the constitution of the Sanhedrin, or highest ecclesiastical council of the Jews.

This body consisted exclusively of elders (Numbers 11:16) chosen from all the tribes of Israel. Those from the tribe of Levi, were, of course, of the priestly office. They added to their function as elders, that of ministers before the altar in the sanctuary. To distinguish them from elders of other tribes, they were called priest-elders, or elders of the priests (2 Kings 19:2; Isaiah 37:2, etc.), and afterwards chief priests, one being taken in later days from each of the twenty-four courses in the temple. We have thus under the old economy "priest-elders" and "people-elders," corresponding with the two classes of elders in the Presbyterian Church at the present day.

These elders ruled in that olden time, not singly, but jointly. No officer in the Jewish Church had any such individual authority as that now exercised by the bishop of an Episcopal diocese, or the presiding elder of a Methodist district. In every city there was a "bench of elders," which held its sessions in the gate, and to which all questions of government were submitted. In smaller cities this court corresponded to a Church Session, in larger ones to a Presbytery. There was, as we learn from Jewish writers, a higher court, composed of not less than twenty-three elders, to which appeal could be had from the decision of the "elders of the gate," corresponding in this respect to our Synod; whilst above all was the Sanhedrin, or ultimate court of appeal, corresponding to our General Assembly.

It will thus appear that the Church under the old dispensation was essentially Presbyterian, that in the setting up of the new dispensation no change in the form of government was needed, and no breach in the continuity of the Church was made, as Archbishop Whately has so admirably said: "It appears highly probably—I might say morally certain—that wherever a Jewish Synagogue existed that was brought, the whole or the chief part of it, to embrace the Gospel, the apostles did not, there, as much *form* a Christian church (or congregation, Ecclesia) as *make an existing congregation Christian* [the italics are his own]; by introducing the Christian sacraments and worship, and establishing whatever regulations were requisite for the newly-adopted faith, leaving the machinery (if I may so speak) of government unchanged, the rulers of synagogues, elders and other officers (whether spiritual or ecclesiastical or both), being already provided in the existing institutions." "And," he continues, "it is likely that several of the earliest Christian churches did originate in this way; that is, that they were *converted synagogues*, which *became* Christian churches as soon as the members, or the main part of the members, acknowledged Jesus as the Messiah…And when they founded a church in any of those cities in which (and such were probably a very large majority), there was no Jewish Synagogue that received the Gospel, it is likely that they would conform, in a great measure, to the same model."[1]

And, as thus the unity of the visible Church, under the two dispensations, appears in this element of Presbytery, which runs through and characterizes its whole polity, so is it with the unity of the Church militant and the Church triumphant; for in that apocalyptic vision which was given to John of the future glory of Christ's redeemed and ransomed Church, there

---

[1] Richard Whately, *The Kingdom of Christ Delineated* (New York: Robert Carter & Bros., 1854), 29ff.

still appear, as the representatives of this same principle of Presbytery, the "four and twenty elders surrounding the throne" [Revelation 4:4, 10]. Well may we give honor to a system which thus vindicates the unity of Christ's witnessing Church under all dispensations, to the end of time and through the cycles of eternity.

Its Superiority as a Basis for the Organic Unity of the Whole Visible Church in the World

It must be evident that a system which shall unite all Christian people in the bond of a common unity must have provision by which, on the one hand, every part of the Church shall be subordinated to the authority of the whole, and by which, on the other, there shall be the utmost protection and security for the rights and liberties of each individual member.

The first element in this unity, due subordination, is secured very perfectly by the system of hierarchy; that which finds its expression in the Church of Rome—but it is a unity in which the rights and liberties of the private member are completely sacrificed to the oppression and tyranny of the governing power. In the system of independency or congregationalism on the other hand, the rights of the individual are secured, except against that most fearful of all despotisms, the despotism of a majority against whose prejudice or passion there is no protection by the right of appeal. But this liberty is at the expense of due subordination. The system of Presbyterianism secures a unity as complete as that of the Church of Rome, and at the same time a protection for the rights of the individual such as is not found in any other system of jurisprudence, either civil or ecclesiastical. For while it is the boast of our civilization that, by our system of appellate courts the humblest citizen may carry his cause from a lower to a higher tribunal, and so receive an award which is free from all taint of local prejudice or personal malice, yet, in fact, the exercise of this right of appeal is limited by its costliness, and only the favored few who have the means to employ counsel and assume responsibility can carry their cause to the Court of Appeals.

But in the Presbyterian Church the humblest and poorest member can have his cause carried, without any expense, from Church Session to Presbytery, from Presbytery to Synod, and from Synod to General Assembly. The ablest counsel in the land is at his service without one cent of compensation or fee, and he may obtain, as is often done, the voice of the whole Church in the decision of a question in which he feels that his rights or his interests are involved.

The Flexibility by Which This System Adjusts Itself to All Stages and Conditions in the Life of the Church

If you should conceive a man with his wife and infant children thrown by shipwreck upon a heathen island, if he be a Christian believer, and his family a Presbyterian family, then he carries with him a complete Presbyterian Church. Upon him, as the head of his house, the office of the Presbytery or eldership devolves. His wife is the deaconess; his children are the baptized members. There is a complete "church in his house." As his sons come to manhood, or heathen men are converted and taught in the way of the Lord, they are admitted by him to share in the office of the Presbytery, but the Church is complete at the very moment when he is thrown upon the island, and there is no other form of church government under which this would be true.

Again, if the whole Christian world were, today, to resolve to come into organic union under a single form of government, there is (with the exception of the Papal, which, as we have seen, secures only the unity of a resistless and remorseless despotism) no system which could be adopted without a strain too severe to be borne, except that Presbyterian system which we have endeavored in these pages to sketch. No Baptist Convention or Congregational Association that could gather in one place could be large enough to represent this whole Ecumenical Church. No Methodist Conference or Episcopal Council, even though they were limited to diocesan bishops, could find a hall large enough for their assembly. But our Presbyterian system, without a strain upon its machinery, would add another to its ascending series of courts, and as now Church Sessions are represented by delegates in Presbyteries, and Presbyteries by delegates in General Assemblies, so General Assemblies would be represented by delegates similarly chosen in an Ecumenical Council, and the unity of the whole visible Church finds expression without a moment's confusion or jar.

There are many other excellencies which we might claim for our Presbyterian system, such as its spiritual power through its peculiar hold upon the family relation, its historic bearing upon the problems of civil and religious liberty, etc. I content myself with a single additional reason for our love and veneration for our time-honored Presbyterianism.

The Historic Associations that Cluster About It

From the days of the apostles until now the Church, in its purest forms, has been Presbyterian. The Waldenses, who, in their native valleys of the Piedmont, maintained the purity of the primitive doctrine and the simplicity of Christian ritual, amidst all the corruptions and superstitions of the Church of Rome, were Presbyterian. Claiming to have received their doctrine and discipline directly from the apostles; refusing to submit to the authority of the Church of Rome; remaining unshaken in their simple faith through all the fires of persecution and of martyrdom; extorting even from their persecutors reluctant but explicit testimony to the simplicity of their piety and the blamelessness of their lives, they maintained the light of a pure Presbyterian doctrine and order through all the darkness of the middle ages, and there, in the secluded valleys of the Piedmont, it was still blazing when Luther and Farel and Zwingli and Calvin kindled on the highest mountain tops the watchfires of the Reformation.

Another witness through these dark ages for a pure Presbyterianism, is found in the church of the ancient Culdees, of Scotland. This church owes its establishment to the labors of Columba, a native of Ireland, who, about the middle of the sixth century went, as an evangelist, into the midst of the Picts of Scotland. Having converted great multitudes of these fierce tribes to Christianity, he established upon the island of Iona a seminary of learning for the training of pastors and evangelists for his work. The ministers trained in this seminary were called Culdees, and the churches founded by them Culdee Churches—the world *Culdee* being most probably a corruption of the Latin words *Cultor Dei*, worshipper of the true God. These churches of the Culdees, or worshippers of God, existed for many centuries without holding any connection with the Church of Rome. Indeed, they not only refused to acknowledge the authority of the Romish See, but they protested against its errors and innovations, and maintained their ground successfully against its usurpations and encroachments until the very dawn of the Reformation. Their form of government was essentially Presbyterian. They had a Synod or Assembly, to the members of which they gave the name of *Seniores*, or Elders. These elders, acting in their collective capacity, elected and ordained to the ministry. All ministers were of equal rank. Those who had permanent charge of churches were called bishops, but their office and authority were simply those of pastors of individual churches. They held no higher rank, and exercised no greater authority than the other *Seniores* who sat with them in council.

We have thus two distinct lines of Presbyterianism running back to apostolic times, and the memories which gather about us today are those of a grand historic Church. Pre-eminently the "Church of the Covenant," her covenants have been sealed with blood. Those primitive martyrs who "were stoned, were sawn asunder," etc., were witnesses for the principles for which we contend today. Those heroic Vallenses who were hunted from crag to crag of their native mountains, who were hurled by their persecutors over the steep precipices and dashed in pieces on the rocks below, were Presbyterians. Those grand old Covenanters of Scotland, who "loved not their lives to the death" for "Christ and His crown," were Presbyterians. This old Church has come down to us with her vesture, like that of her Lord, crimsoned with blood. The most illustrious martyrs, the most renowned confessors, the most valiant reformers have been hers. Let us venerate her for what she has been; let us love her for what she is.

In this centennial year, let us fling forth her encrimsoned banners freshly to the breeze. Let us send forth a larger band of evangelists to carry our standards over rugged mountains, and plant them in sequestered valleys, in rude hamlets and secluded villages. Let us kindle the light of our pure faith and scriptural polity in ever-increasing centers of influence and power. Let us fully endow and equip our denominational institutions of learning, that our young men may be deeply grounded in all those principles for which our forefathers sacrificed and toiled. Let us gird ourselves like men for the work of perpetuating, establishing, and enlarging the sphere of influence of our beloved Church.

And may each one of us so live and so labor that when the testimony of this generation is borne and its work ended, we may transmit to our children, in its purity and in its integrity, the legacy of Presbyterianism which we have received from our sires, having our names honorably linked with the increase of its prosperity, and the enlargement of its influence in the world.